Window for a Small Blue Child

GERRIE FELLOWS was born in New Zealand but now lives in Scotland with her husband and daughter. She trained as a painter at art schools in London and then worked in various countries as a life model, a secretary and a writer in residence. Her first collection, *Technologies and other poems*, was published by Polygon in 1990, followed ten years later by *The Powerlines*. Her third collection, *The Duntroon Toponymy*, was published by Mariscat Press in 2001. Her work has appeared in the anthologies *Intimate Expanses: XXV Scottish Poems 1978-2002*, *Scotlands: Poets and the Nation* (both Carcanet/Scottish Poetry Library, 2004) and *Modern Scottish Women Poets* (Canongate, 2003).

T0167608

GERRIE FELLOWS

Window for a Small Blue Child

CARCANET

First published in Great Britain in 2007 by
Carcanet Press Limited
Alliance House
Cross Street
Manchester M2 7AQ

A CIP catalogue record for this book is available from the British Library
ISBN 978 1 85754 888 4

The publisher acknowledges financial assistance from Arts Council England

Typeset by XL Publishing Services
Printed and bound in England by SRP Ltd, Exeter

for
Tom and Freya
with love

Contents

I

THE INFERTILITY CYCLE

The Lily and the Egg

Are there pictures for this
how the sun falls on them?
The lily on the table by the windowsill
stirs in the draught
the window of the new house
opened with a little push
on to a late summer garden
roses   folded convolutions
of apricot pink   deep, labial

This is the season of the garden
floss flower   potentilla
love-in-a-mist

This is the weather in that garden
days of sun   rain wash
wind raking through the empty space
where there might be bean stalks

Here are male and female in the garden

Aphids gather on the last of the raspberries
dusky red light falls on the garden
Codes pass along neural pathways
hormonal codes enter the bloodstream
The light shines on the late fruit
the dark red berries   *the clustered*
follicles of the ovary secreting oestrogen
The light is golden with the humming of bees
The oestrogen enters the bloodstream

On the window
where the room is reflected
as if it were a garden of growing things
instead of a room with a lily in a vase
someone has traced with her finger
in a writing made of moisture

a signal for the body
The oestrogen has reached the pituitary
Luteinising hormone surges
in a tidal wave of sunshine
The wall of the room thins
the membrane bubbles
the follicle bursts
the egg floats   released
the glass flows in the frame

Inside, the sun
falls on the frilled trumpet
Each filament stirs towards the egg
dehisced into a fluid whisper
What do you see?
They are playing catch
as catch can
as what might be
the lily vase
the egg held in its cupped hands

Birthday Card for the Autumn Equinox

She was born in the spring
on the far side of the world
her body encased oocytes
multiple as stars
locked in meiosis
all across the south
apricot blossom fluttered like nappies
or the blank clean pages of calendars
washed in sunlight, locked in whiteness
waiting for a lifetime
of prewash, boil wash, spinning in cycles
a lifetime of petals and corollas
of oocytes and follicles popping
the world turning and ripening
girls and fruit   turning golden
women and leaves
equinoctial light falling
on her fortieth birthday
tilts the turning hemisphere
towards unencoded space
she falls out of the light
her 400,000 children scatter into stars
in the dark cracked universe

Poem for a Peptide Hormone

Photograph of a house
they do not yet inhabit   for the shapes
they make on the photograph are imaginary
receptors of codes   cracked-open
chain-letters of *amino acids*

A True Copy of Her Last Menstrual Cycle

On day 1
she imagines a room in the roof
on day 5
a stair with windows towards the sky
on day 10
a diagram of construction
divided into summer's corollary of blue
and the meantime she now enters
On day 12
the indistinct colour of the sky
may indicate a dip before ovulation
but on day 13
this is less certain
than the touch of skin hot after sleep
On day 14
the idea of a stair unfolds
into their not yet deconstructed house
On day 15
the forces are vertical
though at this distance it's hard to tell
On day 16
their bodies *resolve*
into their components
normal to and axial along the rafter
On day 17
the roof space is shown on the plan
annotated at a ratio of 1:50
On day 20
she imagines three windows
in which the sky opens
convolvulus blue each morning
On day 25
she spans space with family
constructs children and hope
On day 28
the chart is almost complete
a true copy of the plan referred to
It is not the future they imagined

Oestrogen

Entrant
through water-repellent walls   *lipid-soluble*
visitant to houses and microscopes
cell-binding spellbinder
the rooms wait for and shimmer and wait

A Pink and Blue Poem

I

She buys kits of colours   boxed
instructions   pink wash   to red
run in the wash *doubly marked antibodies*
the pissed-on each morning substance
she collects like butterflies one after another

On day 11
the absorbent sampler shows
the palest chemical pink
On day 12
a sleepsuit/the flush of a baby's cheek
On day 13
wool waiting to be knitted
into a pastel *clumping   a visible precipitate*
On day 14
it's ribbons for babies/booties/celebrations
On day 15
a cradled shawl/a rosebud mouth
On day 16
the cot blanket she'll bed her baby in
dark as the spill of birth

The pictures haunt her   time-
released photographs of sunset clouds
doubly marked
antibody binding to antigen
antigen to substrate
This reading is not false

deep-bedded blood vessels darken
to a blood stain   a sign she took once
as fertility   This reading is false/

II

The ovulation kits turn blue with cold

/but the readings are not false   *they are*
99% accurate   The readings are false
they have a 1% margin of error
The margin is blue   and the readings
are transparent with winter clarity

Hold in the stream of urine
for a few seconds
and on day 12
you will receive the pale blue of a bib
on day 13
the powder blue of a babygro
on day 14
a scrap of sky blue fleece   *the edge*
of a test panel to which
an antigen is bound
on day 15
a line of ocean   the deep blue
surge of *luteinising hormone*
on day 16
the two blue mittens of your child
will wave at you from the surge line

Each month the portholes open
into promises   he loves me/
he loves me not   They are false/
they are not false   they are the blue
of ocean   cobalt   ultramarine/
they are the blue of distance
azure   cerulean

The window fills with frost

A Folk Tale

A boundary of stiff lace   intricacies
of snowflakes   imprinted
like the cut-out faces of children
hushed in the dark of a puppet-show

Steam condenses on a window pane

The snow child melts and vanishes

Information

is what they're after
in this together
in their family doctor's
humdrum familiar room

A day 21 progesterone level
indicative of ovulation

She hopes it works   biochemistry
traced colour in mist
dissemination of knowledge

the past's milky trace   revealed
in microscopic densities of sperm
a dividing line of 20 million/ml

The letter of referral might do the trick
She hears it happens   the body deciding
a quick fix

She's not thinking   waiting list times
she's not thinking   INFERTILE

though they've come
to have their fortunes told
to know the future

Dream Baby (I)

They're studying the blueprints
for a circular kitchen   ash rings
to encompass them as they cook
the radiant structure   a flower
opening and there she is
cute as a baby in a buttercup
Butter glows gold under their chins

Ancestral Luck

This is what happens
one evening: her sister's voice

At the site of follicle rupture
the collagen network melts
the follicle collapses   cells multiply

turning yellow as she drives   a bloom as bright
as the flowers she hasn't thought to bring
dandelions, Welsh poppies folding
and pleating themselves around a cavity
a clotted mass into which blood oozes

An event   as invisible as the ancestral luck
of the heart   or the rupture
of the aorta's intimate bindings

At the end of the journey
her father slipped between life and death
Doctors listen for   *murmurs*
absent pulses   broken
branches of trees sheared off in flight

Lulled by his daughters
on *the smooth waves of the aorta*
straightening   fragmenting
'He's lucky you've so much time,' the neighbour says
'He's lucky you don't have children.'

He will walk out from death   wildly
silver-haired   and free
though he cannot be free of his own heart
pumping its turbulent blood
he must carry it with him into a future
in which *mucopolysaccharides pool*
and muscle fibres are disarranged
in which he will come home changed
into an old man   no one's grandfather

Her Body

half-turned to glass   a window
through which will be visible
assays   appointments   letters of referral
Each ovary   a mosaic globe
scarred with follicles   *grossly*
white-appearing   lost children

In the Shape of a Map

These are the maps that are made
of their bodies   a diagram
of the stars   a chart navigators use

reading an archipelago of stains
a tide pulled by a moon in the hypothalamus
a calendar of rings   popped foil
the body's ebb   the coil
her body recoiled from
a map revealing *no outward signs*
of dysfunction   no lumbering giantess
or secret anatomies: disordered caves
outgrowths of flesh instead of babes

A projection showing *no sign of orchitis*
though orchids have been spotted
growing profusely in a nearby meadow
No tenderness of the prostate
or the seminal vesicles
though he has kissed her as tenderly
as the old songs say
No history of exposure
to aromatic or chlorinated hydrocarbons
though the bedding planes of rocks
are folded in each thin-skinned structure
each landscape of canals
closed loops embedded in a matrix

from which samples will be taken:
semen for analysis
by volume/density/morphology/motility
serum estimations
of gonadotrophin levels

The clues she leaves
are *spinnbarkeit of mucus*   vaginal smear
endometrial biopsy

the biochemical trace in the blood
of *prolactin   thyroxine*
FSH   oestradiol
Day 21 progesterone

These are the maps that are made
of their bodies' secretions
the mixed agglutination reaction
no history of love

A man and a woman
a geography of loss

A Box for Love

Skin gestures
            Layered cells
that fold themselves over chemical tides
over rivers and canals
over sperm ducts
and transient molecular waves

Layered cells
that pulse themselves into bliss
the field where meaning dissolves

A Cytohistoarchitecture

All morning the sun has hammered the house
to a copper heat-haze of rubble and dust
the battened rafters of the roof
the new lining: board and wool and netlon
layers of fibres thick with it

All morning the work of the body:
a wall deconstructed reconstructed
a membrane nailed and glued
a deeper stratum, coiled and convoluted
the red pine stair section by section
angled into place in the thick glazed air

In the blue evening after noise and dust
after the vacuum cleaner has sloughed a path
through debris   an outline of a room
suspended in that bloom of heat
a cavity or a maze of spiralling wants
the endometrium's nestled layers?

Instead of a summer moon
the corpus luteum sheds its yellow light
over the mute earth of the garden
like a flute's sound   the sweet secretion
of the day's heat rises off the soil

Dream Baby (II)

Is it a basket that bobs on the waves
of heat through the glassed porch door
or a peach? It's summer, season of peaches:
the fruit is downy, blooming   fit to burst
A man and a woman slice into it together
and there at its heart is a child
furry with birth   shimmering
beyond their reach in the dream kitchen

Conversation (Blue Tablecloth)

Two women at a table
by a windowsill pink with geraniums
a back court aflame with drowsy blooms
One of them pours tea translucent
as a river or the tidal wash
of mud and blueness at a river mouth

She is three months pregnant
It's safe now to tell

What makes the other lay open her heart
the teapot's golden brew of secrets
the coloured cloth with its sea blues
or through the window after drought
the early scarlet of turning leaves?

'But this is an IVF baby,'
she said, 'I would have done anything.'

In the transmutable garden
scar tissue   flame lesions like vivid petals
late summer rain on shifting griefs

Wish List

For a June baby
a cool north step
the company of neighbours
the wing of a cry

for a child born in July
the dark hair of a Celt
a coastline
and her father's smile

for a girl born in August
an island   pebbles
a flight over water

Though she makes no gifts
out of her own grief
in the summer of births

Blue Mountain Postcard
Six Slides from a Testicular Biopsy

From an altitude of 6,543 metres
this is what he sees:
through the lens *a connective tissue matrix*
of granite and ice
the forked lingam of Shiva

Pathways cleave among rubble
a complex membrane of gullies and rock-fall
mountain debris
shed *from the surface into the lumen*
a journey through glacial moraine
past *outpouchings* of ice
into milk water
rivulets to braided river channel

This is what is seen:
a series of slides
showing *the composition and topography*
of six blue lakes   glacial debris
of the six cellular associations
found repeatedly in the seminiferous tubules

A set of transparencies describing
the colours of flowers
photographed repeatedly on a glacial meadow

The interpretation of data
Stopped time

A Film Made in a Cold Light

She is absent   deep in her body
where nerve endings make no noise
a map on which can be traced
the course of the great rivers
avoidable by a neat incision
below the umbilical rim
a tangential path through layers of skin

A film begins with a light
transmitted through a window
by a bundle of fibres
The light illuminates a wintry field
the nearest moon   white, undulated
perfect with signs of ovulations
a corpus luteum adding its yellow beam
to a landscape glassy with hoar-frost
dense peritubular adhesions
clubbed fimbriae obscured by scar tissue
the wands of luminous grasses

The uterus is the point of reference
in a difficult landscape
images magnified or diminished
A photograph of a lily leaning its bloom
towards the surface of the ovary
is a hand held up to the moon
Methylene blue spilling from one Fallopian tube
a flood the moon shines on
until a hand moves over and blocks it out

Interpretation of what is seen
requires perfect topographical knowledge

This is the director's cut   The film ends

In Answer to the Question, What is Possible?

Tick one of the following boxes:

A skin wound may be closed
with clips, stitches or absorbable suture

A wound may be closed with a butterfly's wing

It is possible you are light-headed

The flap of a wing may ripple the invisible

Window for a Small Blue Child

In the winter garden
floodlit   too cold for snow
flits   beyond tree boles
thin glass branches
a wight   wild blue shadow

Absence

They travel on a road that rises
into night   a crackled silence
beyond the blur of metal and fanned heat
that speeds them beaming light
between luminal constrictions
lakes of blood and fluid that will freeze
before they reach home's orange haze

but the house they enter is immured in chill
their palms slide for switches on its walls
their footsteps are echoes in the unlit
rooms they've chosen to re-inhabit
curtaining the windows with vapour
setting the fug of wine and pasta
against the petrified blue of a garden

whose frost cracks pipes and hearts
(One whole morning her body poured blood)
Now in the kitchen's foggy heat
a cupboard avalanches its burden of jars
the uterine lining disintegrates
in an intimation of catastrophe
a wave of glass and lentils ground sugar

II
THE PELLUCID ZONE

Invocation

They say women
who want children
will do anything
call for benison
fling sacred items
down deep wells
visit the makers
of potions   keepers
of light boxes
to rise up blessed

Ice Baby

A man has cradled his daughter over ice
A woman pushes a pram through banked-up snow
The pram resembles a Petri dish
inside is their baby   thawed
and pink with life   her head a peachy stubble

Picture Show

What she sees are the framed smiles
of other women's babies
glowing advertisements of success
It's safe to look: they have no sound
these babies with their puckered mouths
are photographs   multiple gifts
wrapped in dimples and strawberry hats
glossy with colour and health

They look like promises
in their boxed colours: repeating smiles
like screen-printed images
or television sets in a shop window
the same show played over and over
while she's out in the spring sleet
watching the static form itself
out of pixels   the snow child
turning blue in the spindrift flicker

Numbers and Leaves

She's problem-solving in finite steps:
follicles / oocytes / fertilised zygotes
diminishing until the blank sheet
is thick with *multiple gestations /*
singleton pregnancies / failure to implant
Each box reflecting through a tangle of green
the rates of miscarriage in women over forty
the numbers and leaves of the statistical tree
Some of the windows are fixed and will not open
But this is false   for any window
may be opened and become the future
chromosomal abnormality in twins, in triplets
the risks of amniocentesis to a healthy foetus
The stories inside the house flicker with light
She calculates the chances of *a take-home baby*
the child who waves from just one of those windows
so many rooms inhabited by grief

The Light Box

It begins with her body   it begins
with the intricate embrace
of muscle and fluid
disrupted by a ceramic sliver
transmitting signals as pulsed sound
particles shifting along the path of a wave
reflected echoes the transducer transforms
to a piezoelectric grammar

On the screen a blue movie
a visceral shiver of tissues and space
the invisible made visible   ghostly bindings
transfigured into roped *iliac vessels*
The nurse interpreting the structures
until they become objective parts
darkly moving bladder   cloud-lit ovaries
the inky *echogenic* embrasure of the uterus
each organ   in a series of translations
disembodied to a language of light

Deep blue and flickering with shadows
like the leaves of a tree
her own body she carries in their hands
a box woven of dreams

Infertility Rite I: Body Clock

Five times a day
at four-hourly intervals
the patient is thinking of time
and whether it's time
for a *hormone analogue*
to be administered
Slipping out of a room
before her alarm clock rings
the spray in her handbag
chemically synthesised
her very own spring fragrance
the future delivered in pulses
into her bloodstream
On hormonal pathways
her body's codes   blocked
a chemical trick of the light
fed back as moonshine
Pain she blacks out from

When she comes to
on the bathroom's cold vinyl
the patient is thinking of nothing
its raised honeycomb against her cheek
her husband's voice calling
from the distant noises of the night
She has no idea
how much time has passed

Still Life with Cup

A telephone   cupped
morning light on the cusp
of her stilled hand
about to lift the receiver
on the first day
of blood: spilt

colour that doesn't clot
into knots or blood ties
but dissolves solves puzzles
salves hurt meaning healing
but this menstrual flow
is a fiction   a fake flower
strung by synthetic hormones
on the trellis of a calendar
not lost   looped in the airy lift
quiescent ovaries adrift

her body knowingly deceived

Her hand above the telephone
in this stilled moment

Infertility Rite II: In River Light

She closes the door on the sealed doses
the pharmacopoeia in the fridge
drives the river's concrete span
in a flying light over sheafed water
as if she could take control
of blocked process   tangled tubes

In her handbag her triplet vessels
of holy water   *purified*
from the urine of postmenopausal women
knowingly or unknowingly delivered up
like a prayer on the pilgrim route
to *Assisted Conception*

A rite enacted and re-enacted
in the snap of the ampoules
diluted in solution
in the flick of the young nurse's finger
in her own body   each morning
as *nanograms of oestrogen*

Blood Text

read between her body's scanned tides

translated into layers of meaning
a text revealing what was hidden

in the blood which clots into numbers
the seeded chemistry of the cells

Infertility Rite III: Blue Window

I

Over the far flung reef of visions
the windscreen she scries through
is an intimation of a blueness
the transducer coaxes into image
Her body opening into clusters
microcosms darkling in the fluid hoops of space
the presence and number of follicles
each bubble   magnified
to a shadow on a wall   a shower of inky buds

II

stagelit to the screen's blue flicker
Patient and nurse, each searching for what
they expect to see   *swollen distended ovaries*
(vines heavy with grapes in a blue window)
Nothing is hidden   the body is open:
its outer forms, inner structures
The sister surveys what is there
measuring the endometrium as it thickens
calculates the diameter of each dark follicle
She measures but cannot multiply
'Four,' she says.   'It's not a lot.'

III

A man and a woman at another window
(a window into which evening has fallen
scratching lintels and stanchions
with its blueness) know this may not work
They look out beyond the garden
into a future without children

Who are they   these fictional characters
unlikely inhabitants in a dreamt house
participants in a narrative of delusions?

In the world they live in they make their own luck
They will uproot themselves   outside family
become travellers in their own strange freedoms

Timing   is crucial:

corona cells loosen, turn columnar
'With so few follicles
I have to warn you, there's a risk of failure.'

Such a small harvest   a honeycomb
a beekeeper might comb
each cluster waiting to rupture

and yet   she's as full-bellied
as a woman about to give birth in water
about to be breached and beached

A Map Showing Interior Space

I

She must entrust herself
again to their gloved hands   give up
consciousness and speech
her heavy body: a heavenly body
afloat on a screen   a map
showing *uterine fundus Fallopian tube*
ovary pierced by an aspirating needle
each membrane   each blood-tangled lining
punctured   each oocyte *dehisced*
into a fluid whisper of pale honey
retrieved from what lost place
as if the gynaecologist gathered them
to the lab's glass follicles from empty space

II

Seven oocytes afloat in their bubbled glass
those that were visible and those
that were hidden
beyond the ultrasound's blind echoes
folded in the body
of the woman who wakes now
The sun, she sees, falls on the windowsill
on a lily in a vase
on *an aspirator in a gloved hand*
on the glass that flows in the frame
They are playing catch   as catch can
the oocytes in their medium
with what might be   in a cupped glass

Photomicrograph I

showing the oocyte
surrounded by the zona pellucida
a lit halo in mist

surrounded by
the rays of an exploding star

Cumulus covers the oocyte

The first polar body
visible under the cloud mass

Centrifugal Image

involving his sperm

liquefied / diluted / mixed
separated from the act of love
flown outward

resuspended

spun *repeatedly*
into thin streamers of light

Night Laboratory

In the closed environment of dream
in wombs of glass and serum
possible and impossible babies

multiply until she wakes
stumbling from bed doubled up with pain
puts out a hand to stop herself
tumbling into the dark
in which she knows nothing   not
the thud of her body to the floor
a woman caught sight of
from a helicopter or a passing plane
her husband pushing against a door
that's blocked by the dead weight
of her fallen body

though she's lighter than a vacuum
inhabited by hormones and absence
in these ghostly hours

showing the cloud
on the horizon of the eye
has been dispersed

making visible
a second polar body
extruded into perivitelline space

The zona pellucida
is sealed in a cupped translucent sea
sperm cling to its surface

The photomicrograph shows
the male and female pronuclei
of a fertilised oocyte

The Ghost in the Machine

They wait without knowing
while *pronuclei migrate and fuse*
autistic sleepers counting
the possible hours
picking numbers patterns
replications   sleepwalking
while genetic codes inhabit their skin
and *chromosomes rearrange themselves*

They wait for processes
connections   layers of code
the way the telephone works
her diary beside it and her hand
about to lift   used to this
the voice   disembodied
the ghost in the machine

They think nothing of it   float
bits of themselves into electrical code
trusting to hear some kind of truth
in the signals locking   unlocking
the voice reassembling itself
the stranger saying
'You have four fertilised embryos.'

Photomicrograph III

showing
each of the daughter cells
divided
making four
perfectly formed
symmetrical *blastomeres*
each visible nucleus
implicit with codes
replicating and dividing
and always equal
to forty-six

The collection of cells
known as the zygote
held in the trembling jelly
of their second skin
shivering to cleave
ready to roll and multiply

The Arbor Vitae

The procedure is one of navigation
on branching corridors
to a waiting room
where on the far shore of a divide
the chatter of technicians
goes quiet   and they're exposed
a suspect pair   fallen silent among the wank mags
a couple found guilty of infertility

The journey is what happens
Follow the branches and stems of the tree of life
At each junction make a decision
receive what luck gives you

find yourself in a room without windows
a clinical space
in which *the transfer of three zygotes*
is not contraindicated
by the patient's recent history of pain and blackouts

The procedure involves the aspirations of a couple
and a journey once made by sperm
(propelled in love and lust or duty
or none of the above)
In ancient times they climbed this way
through the arbor vitae
the folds of the cervical lining
like the branches and stems of the tree of life

The procedure involves the aspiration
of three zygotes from their glass cradles
and their transfer   *(transcervically*
using a fine catheter)   into the patient's uterus

The patient is awake
and the zygotes are afloat in the catheter
The catheter is inserted
through the folds of the cervix into her uterus
(there is hardly a prick) *its tip*
is advanced to the fundus   withdrawn slightly
and three little bundles of cells
enclosed in their shimmering skins
are propelled to sink or swim

The procedure takes a matter of minutes
After which the patient is given
two boxes of progesterone pessaries
and a photocopied scrap on which
this story is written:

7 oocytes   4 fertilised
3 embryos replaced
0 embryos stored for future cycles

Box for the Future Tense

Blood determines the meaning
of the time she's waiting in
She answers with meanings of her own
not knowing the levels
of *serum oestradiol, serum progesterone*
she listens to her body
not knowing the levels of *serum hCG*
she is almost pregnant

Intimations

Her body in the mirror
her nipples' dark aureoles
She says nothing   superstitious
as a wife at midnight well
moon-drenched   silence a spell

The Future Tense

I

They're flying south to smiles that bloom
on wedding photos from fifty years ago
progesterone surging from the corpus luteum
canvas lit with small blue flames

Among all these people: family, guests arriving
fragments of speeches and chat
she carries her jelly babies encased, dividing
in the fold of her uterus

Each day that passes and she does not bleed
her hope is a flag she has yet to unfurl
encoded with wonders *chemically evident*
two to three days after implantation

a fairy tale she wants to believe
triumphal, a charmed life   it is possible
the endometrium in a state of heightened activity
if she does not tell it will all come true

Each day that passes: closer to the voice
that'll break the spell cast on her body
progesterone's trick   its false signs
and her own silence

in which an unrequitable grief is embedded

II

Among names and faces, conversations
a series of lacunae appear in the cell mass
a proliferating pattern of stitches and babies
a family in needlepoint: a golden wedding gift

This is what happens: she will bleed

a blot will spread into dark silk onto folding wood
she'll be imprisoned in her loss   struck dumb
at a table bright with a criss-cross of talk
until she rises, makes her way upstairs

This is what happens: *failure to implant*

What is she thinking through the blur of grief?
Try again   we were almost there
the drug regime, the night black-outs
as if this way she could stave off loss

There are no embryos stored for future cycles

Marooned among failed talismans   broken-open
packets of tampons brought to ward off blood
the blues of her dress are the dark she'll fall into
her blood the stifled weeping she can't do

III

Among fragments of speeches and chat
the family network   *layered cells*
from which a future may be forming
she carries her secret attention

a trophoblast extracting nutrients
from endometrial secretions
abstemious as a slimmer in her deep blue
turning down wine, beef, blue cheese

They wait without knowing
if *human chorionic gonadotrophin*
is already measurable in the maternal urine
each day closer to an unrequitable grief

flying home to a voice on the phone

'The test is positive.'   The voice

is cautious, warning   and she knows she shouldn't:
it's early days yet   unpacking her cheap silk dress

flapping it out as if its celebratory ripple
were already unwearably slim   a flag
she's about to fly from her washing line
coded with good luck   the news they can't yet tell

What the Body Promises

Why should she believe she is lucky
that cells are as multiple as stars migrating inwards
galaxies spinning outward?

Why should she believe an embryo ensnares the sun?
She is not yet a statistic
in *clinical pregnancies per IVF cycle*

Why should she believe a head fold curls around a heart tube?
Why should she believe in the gills of a fish?
Her chances of miscarriage may be 40%

Why should she believe her belly's queasy ocean
her breasts' dark moons
Why should she believe in the glow of light on her skin
or her hair's lustre
before the ultrasound's flickering codes?

Why should she believe the story her body tells her?
The risks of ectopic pregnancy in a damaged tube
a gynaecological emergency

The blue window may reveal nothing but echoes
of lost embryos   children scattering into stars
in the dark cracked universe

The blue window may reveal *a multiple gestation*
nestled cookies of misfortune   tiny sick babies

Why should she believe in the future tense?
Nothing is promised

Image for a Sonar Room

A blue window with a curtain
sunlight on a stalk attached to a flower
the petals and corolla of the sonar room
and beyond it her body with what it knows

III

THE FLOWERINGS OF THE POSSIBLE

I

Who are they   these fictional characters
are they ourselves
as we were then before our daughter
became human in my body
and entered the world?

Participants in a narrative
through which real women and men
are driven   or choose to enter
putting themselves into fiction
into that blue space
in which hope and delusion jostle

A couple *desperate* for children
the word used   as if
rising unbidden it must be true
Were we desperate   outlaws from family
wanderers who'd left it too late to settle down?
We could have lived through loss
beyond it   other lives were possible
even the one we'd lived
with its small adventures and daring
its mountain solitudes   the self's
attention to the moment   a step
in air from one country to another

II

'I know I'm setting myself up for grief,' I said
But grief's what might have been

'If we'd no money,' he said 'this would be the end.'
But we'd enough
for two attempts, maybe three

and we were lucky   blessed
is the old, worshipful word for it
Our daughter's photo
on the consulting room wall
became one of those seeming promises
like the one this fairy story makes
adding its smiling picture to the burden of hope

Do you imagine the story ended here in a blue room
with the pulse of a baby's heart
or with those photographs?

The pictures are not what happens:
though the babies are real
(the nurses' real joy, the doctors' pleasure)
they do not show
the ovaries bloated, blood losing fluid
thickening to a clot   or years later
the uncertainties of cells mutated

They do not show
a woman's womb scanned
for a heartbeat that's irretrievable
or the yearned-for pulse
deadly in a Fallopian tube

They do not show
the twins born before term
or the pregnancies intruded upon
by scan after scan
the monitored births of *precious babies*

IV

Years later, walking downhill
with another woman
in a rain-sparkled evening

it's as if we've both been waiting
until we're alone to talk
the where, the how, the how many

'We've never said.   Even now
we've friends who must still think
we just never wanted children.'

Three hours ago we were strangers
Now at the subway entrance
we kiss one another in recognition

and she walks away into her life
as once she walked away
from the web of almost   saying
'No, it's taking over my life.'

A long time ago now her grief and loss
She has no child   she lives
those other flowerings of the possible

V

Walking away from the hospital
with our new-born daughter
(after all the scans   all those blue
moons made of her body and mine)
we were released from medicine
into the life of the world
into our lives together

in this house
that's choc-a-bloc

with the made and the found
the strewn garden   the back steps
she comes whooping up trailing sand
inhabiting our lives with friends and games
with back-chat and buttery fingers
with rage laughter music
turned up   full volume
the life of my daughter

How lucky we are   Even now
a phrase cast by a dance club teacher
's a ribbon rippling the air between us
'She's just great. You're lucky to have her.'

Yes, I think   and how

VI

close it was
and how lucky we are
who did not come to grief
or only that lesser grief
of watching other women pregnant
with their second babies   their third
How easy it seems for them   a family
(What do I know of another woman's hope
miscarried   I who never lost a child?)
seeing only her cluster of children
bonded in rivalry and love   the siblings
my daughter will never have
another woman's house full of children

When my daughter comes to rest
she draws: this time a crowded bus
a face in each window   and all of them
wildly grinning
from red pencilled ear to ear
the whole bus choc-a-bloc with children

How luck may visit us: the friend
with eighteen follicles at the first attempt
trying without success for a second child:
How grief is a door we can keep opening

VII

At forty-one I lived through weeks
with the chance of pregnancy
balanced in my body
against the risk of triplets

One of those embryos became my daughter
The others *(their perfect membranes*
their unfragmenting, even cells)
are her lost siblings
hazarded beginnings   embedded
only in fluid   flushed out
or decaying: My body did this
but not my body alone

And what of the other   the one
not chosen   *allowed to perish*
and the unfertilised oocytes
not to be used in any project of research
the waste products of conception
the clinical waste of the lab

as if the body had become gigantic
and embryologists had taken the place
of its thinking cells
the wise and fallible happenstance
of a woman's body
over possible and impossible lives?

VIII

In a house above a blue harbour
I sat at dinner with a grandmother
of IVF twins born too early
How hard this is   her daughter's
love   her grandchildren's struggle
She did not say   it might have been better
Grief is a door we can keep opening
Instead she said
'You were lucky, having just the one.'

IX

'What are you writing?' my daughter asks me
and I tell her   'The story
of a man and a woman
who wanted a child'   explain again
my body's damaged tubes
the taking out   the putting back
But she does not want this detail
It's history   a past
her mother and father lived through
She shrugs it off:
after all, don't all babies get made
from a sperm and an egg?
She raises one eyebrow at me
and dances off, singing full volume
into her own childness   her presence

Glossary

Antibody: A defensive protein produced in response to the action of a foreign body.

Antigen: A substance which provokes the production of a specific antibody. This can be used to detect the presence of a particular hormone, for example, in an ovulation test and is the process which forms the basis of the hormone assay.

Arbor Vitae: The tree of life. The folds of the cervical lining, so called because of the ancient belief that sperm climbed the treelike folds towards the uterus.

Aspiration: The ultrasound-guided process of sucking out the eggs and the follicular fluid from the ovarian follicles with a very fine hollow needle.

Blastomere: The cells of the fertilised ovum or zygote, are known as blastomeres.

Clinical Pregnancies per IVF Cycle: Pregnancy confirmed by a heartbeat seen on a scan. Clinical pregnancy rate per treatment cycle is one of the statistics Assisted Conception units are legally required to publish.

Cold Light: The fibre optic light used in laparoscopy does not produce heat.

Corona Cells: The corona radiata, a layer of cells attached to and radiating outwards from the maturing ovum. Prior to ovulation these cells become columnar and looser.

Corpus Luteum: Literally, yellow body – the ovarian follicle after the egg is released changes into the corpus luteum which then produces progesterone, the hormone which supports the lining of the womb and allows early pregnancy to establish.

Cytohistoarchitecture: The cellular tissue structure.

Dehisced/Dehiscence: The gaping open of an ovarian follicle allowing the oocyte and follicular fluid to ooze out.

Ectopic Pregnancy: A pregnancy implanted outside the uterus, most commonly in a Fallopian tube – it can be a complication of IVF treatment in a woman with damaged tubes. It can also occur in natural conceptions.

Endometrium: The lining of the uterus.

Fallopian Tube: The delicate, open-ended tubes along which eggs travel from the ovary to the womb, and in which fertilisation would normally take place. Blocked or damaged tubes are a major cause of infertility.

Fimbriae: Fingerlike structures at the open end of the Fallopian tube which move across the surface of the ovary to catch the egg.

Flame Lesions: Endometriosis: a condition where endometrium develops outside the uterus. A cause of infertility.

Follicle: The sac-like structure in the ovaries containing oocytes.

Follicle-stimulating Hormone (FSH): A hormone secreted by the pituitary, which stimulates growth of oocytes in the ovarian follicles.

Fundus: The inner surface of the dome of the uterus, between the Fallopian tubes.

Gonadotrophins: The follicle-stimulating hormone (FSH) and luteinising hormone (LH).

Human Chorionic Gonadotrophin (hCG): A hormone secreted by the placenta to support the corpus luteum. It is produced only in pregnancy and its presence in the urine is the basis of pregnancy tests.

Human Menopausal Gonadotrophins (hMG): After the menopause high levels of the hormones FSH and LH are produced. These can be extracted from urine and purified for use in infertility treatment to stimulate the development of follicles: the so-called 'fertility drugs'.

Idiopathic: Without apparent external cause, unexplained infertility.

Iliac Vessels: The large arteries and veins which supply and drain the pelvic region and the legs.

IVF (In Vitro Fertilisation): Literally, in glass, a reference to the Petri dishes in which oocytes and sperm are incubated and in which fertilisation takes place. Generally, used to describe the whole process of fertility treatment in which a woman is stimulated to produce multiple eggs which are aspirated from the ovaries before ovulation. The oocytes are incubated and mixed with sperm and after fertilisation up to two (previously three) pre-embryos are transferred to the woman's uterus. From oocyte collection to the return of pre-embryos to the woman's body takes about forty-eight hours.

Laparoscopy: The 'keyhole' operation. In infertility tests this is a primary investigation into the condition of Fallopian tubes, ovaries and uterus.

Lipid-soluble: Fat-soluble. A feature of the steroid hormones such as oestrogen.

Lumen: The inside of any tube, for example, the Fallopian tubes or the seminiferous tubules.

Luminal: Pertaining to the lumen.

Luteinising Hormone (LH): The hormone which stimulates ovulation and the production of the corpus luteum.

Meiosis: The process of reduction of chromosomal material in sperm and oocytes at a certain stage of development. The first meiotic division of the single-celled primary oocyte begins in the unborn foetus but is not completed until just before ovulation when the oocyte divides into the secondary oocyte and the first polar body, each with only twenty-three single chromosomes – so that twenty-three pairs of chromosomes can be produced by the fusion of secondary oocyte and spermatozoon.

Methylene Blue: A dye injected into the uterus during laparoscopy. If the Fallopian tubes are patent the dye will be seen spilling from their open ends (see **Tubal Patency**).

Mixed Agglutination Reaction: A test for the reaction of sperm and vaginal mucus, used in infertility investigations. It measures antibodies to sperm.

Mucopolysaccharides: Important structural materials in the body, forming the basis of many connective tissues.

Nanograms per Millilitre: A thousand millionth of a gram per millilitre.

Oestrogen: One of the steroid hormones secreted by the ovaries. Together with progesterone, it stimulates the development of the endometrium. There are many different forms of oestrogen in the body.

Oocyte: An egg from the ovarian follicles. Initially a single-celled primary oocyte which divides to form the secondary oocyte. After the entry of a spermatozoon it becomes the female pronucleus which then fuses with the male pronucleus to form the zygote or pre-embryo.

Orchitis: Inflammation of testicles, often as a result of mumps contracted after puberty.

Orgafol: A trade name for hMG.

Peptide Hormone: Follicle-stimulating hormone and luteinising hormone are both peptide or protein hormones. They are long-chain molecules of amino acids linked by peptide bonds. Peptide hormones interact with receptor sites on the surface of the cell. See also **Steroid Hormone**.

Peritubular Adhesions: Bands of fibrous tissue which have twisted or stuck down the Fallopian tubes.

Perivitelline Space: The space within the vitelline membrane of the oocyte, into which the polar bodies (see below) are extruded.

Piezoelectricity: Electricity produced in certain crystals such as quartz when mechanical pressure is applied. It produces the high frequency waves that are the basis of ultrasound.

Polar Body (first, second): Just before ovulation, the oocyte divides into two cells: the first polar body and the secondary oocyte. Once the fertilising spermatozoon has penetrated the zona pellucida, the secondary oocyte divides again, into the fertilised ovum and a second polar body.

Progesterone: The hormone produced after ovulation by the corpus luteum, which prepares the lining of the uterus for a fertilised egg.

Prolactin: The hormone responsible for lactation. An over-production of prolactin interferes with the hormonal regulation of the menstrual cycle.

Seminiferous Tubules: Microscopically fine tubes coiled in each testicle. Spermatozoa are produced from cells in their walls.

Spinnbarkeit: The elasticity of mucus at ovulation. It should be sufficiently stringy for sperm to be able to travel through it.

Steroid Hormone: A hormone which enters a cell and acts directly on it. Oestrogen is a steroid hormone.

Thyroxine: A hormone produced by the thyroid gland which controls metabolic rate. Thyroid disorders are associated with infertility.

Transducer: The handheld device which emits and receives ultrasound waves.

Trophoblast: The outer layer of the blastocyst (the embryo at eight days after fertilisation) from which the placenta will be formed.

Tubal Patency: Assessment of whether the Fallopian tubes are open or obstructed.

Zona Pellucida: The clear membrane which surrounds and protects the oocyte, and which becomes impervious after the entry of a spermatozoon.

Zygote: The pre-embryo at a very early stage of development. After the entry of a spermatozoon, the secondary oocyte becomes the female pronucleus which fuses with the male pronucleus to form the zygote.

Notes and Acknowledgements

There have been many small changes in IVF procedures since my own experience in the 1990s. Local rather than general anaesthetic is now the norm during follicle aspiration by ultrasound-directed transvaginal retrieval. In order to avoid multiple gestations, the law now limits to two the number of embryos that may be replaced.

The sequence is based on my own experience but has been illuminated by conversations with other women. Several books stand out as particularly enlightening: Sarah Franklin's *Embodied Progress: a Cultural Account of Assisted Conception* (Routledge, London, 1997) and Margarete Sandelowski's *With Child in Mind: Studies of the Personal Encounter with Infertility* (University of Pennsylvania Press, Philadelphia, 1993). A performance by Pavla's Puppets of *The Snow Child* inspired 'A Folk Tale' and the echoing of that motif that occurs throughout the sequence.

The sequence makes reference to a number of textbooks, most notably *Gynecologic Endocrinology*, ed. Jay J. Gold II and John B. Josimovich (4th edition, Plenum Publishing Company, New York; London, 1987); *Gynaecology by Ten Teachers*, ed. Geoffrey V.P. Chamberlain (16th edition, Edward Arnold, London, 1995) and *Basic Science in Obstetrics and Gynaecology: A Textbook for MRCOG Part II*, ed. Sir John Dewhurst, Michael de Swiet and Geoffrey V.P. Chamberlain (Churchill Livingstone, Edinburgh, 1986). 'A Film Made in a Cold Light' owes something also to Luis A. Cibils' *Gynecologic Laparoscopy: Diagnostic and Operatory* (Lea & Febiger, Philadelphia, 1975). For the poem 'Ancestral Luck', I consulted *Aortic Aneurysms: Pathophysiology, Diagnosis and Treatment* (Tatsuzo Tanabe, Hakkaido University School of Medicine, Sapporo, Japan, 1993) and *Lecture Notes on Cardiology* (Aubrey Leatham, C. Bull, M.V. Braimbridge, Blackwell Science, Oxford, 1991).

My thanks go to the other women whose experience of IVF has enlightened my own; to the Scottish Arts Council for the Writer's Bursary during 2003-4 which allowed me to concentrate on writing the sequence; to Elizabeth Burns, John Burnside, Vicki Feaver, Tom Leonard, Gerry Loose and Robyn Marsack for their reading of the poems, and to Dr Robin Yates for checking the glossary for me. Any errors remain my own.

'Conversation (Blue Tablecloth)' is for Louise; 'Ice Baby' for Nick, Louise and Isla. 'Wish List' is for Catherine, Caitlin and Amy.

'Numbers and Leaves' was published in *Images of Women*, ed. Myra Schneider and Dilys Wood (Second Light/Arrowhead Press, Durham, 2006).